Say, Hon...
The Organized Pastor's Wife

Say, Hon...
The Organized Pastor's Wife

by
Dana Pride

Everlasting Publishing
Yakima, Washington
USA

Say, Hon...
The Organized Pastor's Wife
by Dana Pride

All scripture quotations are from
the King James Version

ISBN: 978-1-7348047-5-1

First Edition
Everlasting Publishing
PO Box 1061
Yakima, Washington 98907
USA

Dedication

This book is dedicated to my husband, who beautifully guided my transformation from a diligent church worker to an organized pastor's wife.

Who can find a virtuous woman? for her price is far above rubies.
The heart of her husband doth safely trust in her, so that he shall have no need of spoil.

Proverbs 31:10-11

Contents

House and riches are the inheritance of fathers: and a prudent wife is from the Lord.

Proverbs 19:14

IS THIS BOOK FOR YOU?

Not every woman can be a pastor's wife. A pastor's wife must understand that your husband has been called by God for a specific duty, to share the Word of God, and that God has selected you to help him do his job the best he can, by having your time and your home organized so he can focus on the task God has called him to do. Since his is the pastor of a congregation, he may be expected to be the head of every committee, as well as visit the sick and run the business of the church.

If you are a pastor's wife who does not yet have things in your life organized, you may feel discouraged, incapable, incompetent, and overwhelmed by the expectations placed upon you. This book is for you, to help you to be the best helpmate you can be to your husband. Maybe you feel like you are somewhat organized, but your plans get upset often by those last-minute requests from your husband. Mine come in the form of, "Say, Hon, can you just..." so I need to be ready to squeeze in extra tasks without having to stay up all night to complete the things I need or want to do.

In the case where your husband is the pastor of a church where all members and officers attend regularly, and your husband has plenty of resources available when officers are sick or on vacation, and you are never called upon to step up or fill in; or if you already have your entire life organized, this book might not be for you.

This book is for those of you who never seem to have enough time to do the things on the list your husband (or the church) gives you, so then you can't get to your own list, so then you get in the habit of doing the bare minimum and things don't get finished, things get lost, and you are not satisfied with your own performance. God expects the best of you, and you know you can do a better job, if you just have the right tools available. You long to just get things in order - get your life in order - so you can begin to manage. I hope and pray that this book can help you get started in this perpetual challenge. Your life will bring glory to God when you organize the best way you can, and then let Him lead you in everything you plan and do.

> *And the Lord God said, It is not good that the man should be alone; I will make him an help meet for him.*
>
> *Genesis 2:18*

A UNIQUE POSITION

The pastor's wife often has many roles in addition to being a wife and mother. You may be seen as one of the mothers or the mother of the church. You may hold a position in the church, and/or you may be called to fill in for other church workers who are absent or otherwise do not fulfill their duties, or when a position is vacant, such as secretary, church clerk, treasurer, usher, janitor, counselor, Sunday School teacher, Bible Studies teacher, musician or choir director. This means you need to be familiar the duties of each position so you can be available to assist when your husband needs help. It sometimes seems, the smaller the church, the more that is expected from the pastor's wife. You may also hold a job outside the church, as I have always done, in which case, a chunk of time every week is not your own.

Do all things without complaining and disputing, that you may become blameless and harmless, children of God without fault in the midst of a crooked and perverse generation, among whom you shine as lights in the world, holding fast the word of life, so that I may rejoice in the day of Christ that I have not run in vain or labored in vain.

Philippians 2:14-16

Even if your church has a church secretary, your husband probably needs a personal secretary as well, to take care of matters that come to the home, such as phone calls, visitors, and paperwork he brings home. You are your husband's confidante, defender, protector, and main source of encouragement. When I say 'protector,' I mean when he is resting or working or praying or preparing a sermon, you should be ready to protect him from intrusions, by phone or at the door, at home or in his home office. (Most pastors I know have an office at church as well as an extension office at home, for studying, overflow and urgent matters.)

Whether or not you want to be one, you are an example, not only to the members of your church, but to your family, your community, your neighbors, and your co-workers. You have a lot of expectations on you, to always be gracious, thoughtful, spiritual, kind, mild-mannered, and friendly. You may be criticized for dressing too boldly or too plain; for being too quiet or too noisy; for being too aloof or too nosy; for wearing too much make up or not enough make up; for taking on too many duties for the church, or not doing enough for the church; for not being involved enough in the community, or for spreading yourself too thin in the community, and not available enough for church matters. When you are reprimanded for giving someone a 'side-hug' instead of a 'frontal hug,' you must take it with a smile, and not with an argument or defense. Your attitude will reflect on your husband and on his ministry, and may have an effect the congregation and their attitude towards Christ.

Everything you do is to be done with joy.

Your level of organization will affect your entire family, as well as the congregation you serve.

My voice shalt thou hear in the morning, O Lord; in the morning will I direct my prayer unto thee, and will look up.

Psalm 5:3

1. ORGANIZE YOUR SPIRITUAL LIFE

The first and most important thing is to be sure you are saved: you have accepted Jesus Christ as your personal Savior, and you have a current, active relationship with Him. Confess your sins to Him, and ask for His forgiveness.

Are you sure you are a Christian? How can you know for sure? Before we go any deeper, you need to know that you are a Christian, because the organizational skills I have outlined in this book depend on your decision for Christ. Your life, your focus, must be centered around God and His Son, Jesus.

What is the definition of a Christian? Not merely someone who is born into a Christian home, not a person who does good deeds or who is always serving others. Not someone who goes to church every week; that is merely a religious person. A good person can be and do all of those things without being a Christian.

A Christian is a person who has taken on the character of Christ by accepting Jesus as your personal Lord and Savior. When you accept the gift God has given you, His Son, and begin to live with His Spirit within you, you are a Christian. The Holy Spirit leads and guides you in all you do, inside and outside of the church.

You can be sure without a doubt that you are a Christian. The Bible tells us in Romans 10:9, *"if thou shalt confess with thy mouth the Lord Jesus, and shalt believe in thine heart that God hath raised him from the dead, thou shalt be saved."*

You WILL be saved. It doesn't say you might be saved, or if you do this and that along with it, you will be saved. It says if you declare it and you believe it, you WILL be saved. After you have prayed from your heart the prayer of salvation, you are saved. If you have not yet prayed this prayer from your heart, or if you have any doubts about whether or not you are a Christian, and you truly believe Romans 10:9, you can pray the prayer right now:

"I confess to GOD that I am a sinner. I believe that the LORD Jesus Christ is the Son of GOD. I believe He died on the cross for my sins, and He was raised from the dead by GOD for my justification. I now receive Him and confess Him as my personal Savior."

Congratulations! You are now a child of God, with all the rights and privileges of every other Christian. You have the Holy Spirit living inside you, and you have received the gift of eternal life.

"For God so loved the world, that he gave his only begotten Son, that whosoever believeth in him should not perish, but have everlasting life." – John 3:16

If you are already saved, be sure you are regularly cleansed through His Word.

"That he might sanctify and cleanse it with the washing of water by the word, That he might present it to himself a glorious church, not having spot, or wrinkle, or any such thing; but that it should be holy and without blemish." – Ephesians 5:26-27

It is very important for you to have a good working knowledge of the Bible. You need to be prepared to teach a class when a teacher is absent and be ready with a Biblical answer when asked a question of a spiritual nature.

Set a time every day to meet with God. Make a schedule for reading your Bible. Many Bibles have a reading/study plan in them. You may choose to follow a radio program, such as "Thru the Bible," as I do, but if you do follow any program, be sure it is Biblically based. You must read the Bible for yourself, to be sure the program is accurate and complete. Pray before you begin to read your Bible, and ask the Lord to show you what He wants you to know. He has a new treasure for you inside His Word each day. It's up to you to go treasure hunting to find it. He will guide you to it.

You must be secure in your relationship with Jesus before you can be secure in any other relationship, even marriage, and especially marriage to a pastor. A pastor's wife is a particular target of the devil, because if he can get you off track enough to drive a wedge between you and your husband, the ministry will suffer. The congregation will shift their focus from Jesus to taking sides on the struggle between the two of you, and the world outside the church will get the idea that there is no advantage to being a Christian, since married couples outside the church may seem to be getting along better than those who profess to be Christians. Like it or not, your marriage is an example to others inside and outside the church.

Organize your spiritual life, and everything else will follow.

The heart of the prudent getteth knowledge; and the ear of the wise seeketh knowledge.

Proverbs 18:15

> *Let all things be done
> decently and in order.*
>
> *1 Corinthians 14:40*

2. GET YOUR PURSE IN ORDER

I was carrying around a huge purse with everything I thought I would ever need in it. Did someone need a pen? I've got one. How about a tissue? Yep, I have a pack. What about a breath mint? I know there's one in here somewhere, let me find it... there it is... no, that's not it... wait... okay! Here you go.

I knew my purse was out of control one day when I heard my daughter telling a stranger, "My mom collects pens. She has a pen collection."

"I do not!" I protested, feeling offended that she would think I collect such a mundane item.

"How many pens do you have in your purse?" she asked, her eyes wide with curiosity.

I didn't think I had that many, until I counted them: forty-two! I had 42 pens in my purse! I also had note pads, two pencils, candy, several kinds of mints, gum, Band-Aids, lotion, lip balm, a mirror, erasers, liquid paper, tape, a little camera (this was before cell phones), my check book, lots of loose change, my wallet, a pocket Bible, a small Bible dictionary, several sets of keys, empty candy and gum wrappers, and about a hundred receipts from purchases I had made.

All of these things did not need to be in my purse!

The day after the pen collection remark, I was leaving church to go to my car, and a male church member offered to help me carry some things. When he grabbed the strap of my purse to lift it, he quickly dropped it and commented, "They say women are the weaker sex, but if that's true, how can they lift a purse like this?" He left it for me to carry as he picked up the rest of my items. I knew I had to do something about this purse!

I arrived at home that day with a new priority: I had to organize my purse, right now! I dumped out everything on the table and began to sort things into three piles: what I needed to carry in my purse, what I needed to keep but not in my purse, and garbage. The sorting process took about 45 minutes. What was left for me to carry fit into a much smaller purse. I wanted everything inside my purse to be organized, so I used several pouches to organize items: one pouch for loose change, one for mints and gum, and a tall, skinny one for pens. (It only holds 6 pens, so I selected my favorite ones, and I carry only those.) Fortunately, I had some other purses in my closet, a variety of purses I still liked but my stuff had outgrown, and I selected an appropriate one for my new downsized purse.

When I finally got my purse organized, I felt like my whole life's organization was following its lead. My purse was so light! I no longer had to dig for a pen, a scrap of paper, a cough drop. I never again would hold up the line at the grocery store while I searched for my check book. My purse no longer looked like a pack rat lived inside it, and I knew I had taken my first step to the organized life I need to do my best.

Easy tips for organizing your purse:

• Decide what is essential in your purse and remove everything else.

• Choose the right size for your purse. The bigger your purse, the more non-essential items will soon fill it up.

• Use dividers or pouches to organize the inside of your purse. You will feel a sense of relief each time you are able to find what you need quickly.

But let all those that put their trust in thee rejoice: let them ever shout for joy, because thou defendest them: let them also that love thy name be joyful in thee.

Psalm 5:11

3. GET YOUR CONTACTS IN ORDER

Family, friends, neighbors, church members, pastors, other churches, and community leaders... so many names, phone numbers, and addresses that need to be organized. I had a small family before I was married, and I had their phone numbers and addresses memorized. When my husband and I got married, I became part of his very large family, as well as responsible for phone numbers and addresses of many church members who were also our friends. At Christmas, we were expected to send cards to other pastors and church congregations, as well as to our family and friends. My address book grew from about 20 entries to well over 500! There was no way for me to memorize so many addresses and phone numbers. I could hardly remember all those names without a list!

Note pads with addresses and phone numbers added in a random order, and a stack of scraps of papers and business cards were not the way to go, but that was how it started. How much time did I spend going through piles of little notes and business cards to find a phone number or address? Too much. I needed an organization solution.

I began using an address book, an actual little book, where I kept alphabetized contact information for family and friends. I purchased a separate book for church contacts who were also friends. (This was by no means the church roster or church visitors list – that information was kept at the church.) This got to be confusing, since church members became friends and friends became church members; so I decided to combine all our contacts into one book and indicated in the margin friends with a turquoise 'F,' neighbors with a pink 'N,' and church members with a purple 'C' (my favorite colors).

Every time I sent out family newsletters or birthday cards, and every year after I mailed our Christmas cards, some were returned, due to changed addresses. People move all the time!

And they don't normally send me a change of address notification! When I was using a real address book, I took blank address labels, wrote on them the new addresses, and stuck those over the previous addresses. This kept the entries in alphabetical order.

After a few years of pasting new labels over old addresses (and some entries became very thick with changes), I began using a contacts database on my home computer. One advantage to this was that I only needed one database for all the addresses. I have field entries for 'church,' 'family,' 'friend,' 'neighbor' and 'business,' to differentiate our contacts. I have a check box for 'Christmas,' so I can easily filter for those who receive a Christmas card. I also can search for a specific address or phone number.

Another advantage to using a database for contacts is the ability to print address labels and return address labels – no more hand-writing of envelopes! Although some people may think this takes away the personalization, when you are sending hundreds of cards, this saves so much time, perhaps hours, and reduces the chance of making errors. We later bought a printer that is able to print the addresses and our return address directly on the envelopes – another big time-saver.

When we receive a returned card or letter due to an expired address, I update the database. An out-of-date database is not of much use. It's important to keep it up to date, even when that means calling, texting or emailing friends and family who have moved, to ask them their new address.

One more advantage of having contact information in a database, you can print out phone lists. This is very helpful for us, as we keep a list of our neighbors on the wall near our landline. My husband keeps a printed list of all the phone contacts in his briefcase, since doesn't want the number of every person in the database to be in his cell phone contacts.

Unfortunately, my contacts database on my computer does not sync with my contacts in my phone, so I need to maintain those separately, and remember to update both places when a phone number changes. Again, I stress the importance of keeping your contacts up-to-date.

If you are not familiar with databases, or

you find they are too expensive, you can use a spreadsheet. Entries in a spreadsheet can be sorted and filtered, and you can create layouts for address labels and envelopes.

Organize your contacts, either in a book, a database or spreadsheet, and keep them up to date. As a pastor's wife, you will find this to be a huge time-saver, especially when your husband asks you for a rarely-used number.

My help cometh from the Lord, which made heaven and earth.

Psalm 121:2

4. CALENDARS & BIRTHDAYS

I have learned that it is best to keep one calendar for everything. At one time, we had a calendar in the kitchen for church and community events and a calendar in our bedroom for birthdays and personal appointments. This became a problem when we would check one calendar and not the other, and when several events were happening at the same time. One morning, I called my husband to ask how his doctor appointment had gone, and he replied, "It wasn't on the calendar." Well, he had checked the kitchen calendar and noticed the church events for the evening, but he hadn't looked at the bedroom calendar. This was when I decided we needed one calendar for all events. We keep it in the bedroom, since visitors don't need to see our personal appointments – and they can't add events without us knowing (yes, that has happened).

On Sunday evening, I review the calendar and mention any appointments or unusual activities to my husband, so he is aware of what is happening that week. He also reviews the calendar, but I make it a point to remind him in advance, at the beginning of each week. It is not helpful on Wednesday to notice that he had an appointment scheduled for Tuesday.

You also need a calendar at the church to plan for and keep track of events and birthdays, but, unless you are the church secretary (which I was, temporarily, for 20 years) or event planner, someone else should be maintaining it. I would suggest that you review it at the beginning of each month, to be sure it is in line with your calendar at home.

Regarding birthdays and occasions that call for cards: purchase a variety of cards (birthday, sympathy, get well, thank-you, congratulations, and blank) and keep them handy. I use a small file cabinet with sections for each kind of card. Set a time at the beginning of the month to prepare cards for the birthdays coming up in the following six weeks. I look at the calendar, choose the card for each person, and address the envelopes. Then I prepare the cards by writing an encouraging note and signing them, and often enclose a photo or two. I keep the prepared cards in my designated slot for outgoing mail and send them during the first week of the month. (People don't mind receiving birthday cards early.)

I also take note of graduations and weddings coming up, so I can get those cards prepared on time. Get well and sympathy cards need to be sent as the occasions occur, so it's a good idea to have a variety on hand. As a pastor's wife, you will most likely be sending more cards than the average person, since you have contacts in the church and in other congregations who will be blessed when you reach out to them by mail. This is another time when your organized addresses will come in handy (see Chapter 3).

Do not be discouraged when you send out a multitude of cards and receive very few in return. Most people no longer communicate by mail, but to me, it's important to send cards. This is a part of your ministry of encouragement. When you reach out with a card, your thoughtfulness can be very reassuring to a hurting or lonely person or family, and they have that card to remind them you are thinking of them and praying for them.

Some years back, I received a phone call from an elderly aunt who thanked me for the cards and photos I had sent to her years earlier. She told me she had lost several close friends in a short period of time, and my cards had meant the world to her, even though she had never responded to me by mail. Your small act of kindness sent in a card or letter can lift up an aching soul.

Also- be sure to stay stocked up on stamps, so you will always be ready to send a card at the last minute.

Organizing your calendar and birthdays will help the rest of your life, including your time, to be organized.

She looketh well to the ways of her household, and eateth not the bread of idleness.

Proverbs 31:27

5. ORGANIZING YOUR TIME

Time with God (see Chapter 1) comes first. The best time to plan to spend with God is early in the morning, before kids and dogs and phones and visitors and household duties and your job, if you have one, begin to intrude on your time. As I mentioned earlier, I have held an outside job for the entire time I have been married to my husband-pastor, so my remaining time is precious. I have to admit, it is not easy for me to get up early for anything. Yet, I discovered that if I wait to read my Bible at bedtime, I usually don't get very far before I fall asleep – not necessarily due to the content I am reading, but more because of my physical condition. I am usually plum tired by the time I lie down. I keep my Bible handy, next to my bed. When I first wake up, it reminds me of my top priority – spending time with God. I make it a practice to read a section of the Word before

I do anything else. Then when I am driving to work, I listen to my Bible studies program, which is 26 minutes long, (I'm sure it is not a coincidence) the amount of time it takes me to drive to work.

After Bible studies, it's a great practice to look at your calendar (see Chapter 4) to see what is happening today and this evening, so you know and can inform the rest of your family of any appointments and expectations for the day. This way, things won't sneak up on anyone. You will be ready for anything, including the added duties that often pop up without warning. "Say, Hon, can you just type up this letter before you go?" "Say, Hon, can you just make a little flier for next month's revival?" "Say, Hon, can you call and check on Mother Smith, to see if her daughter is out of the hospital?" "Say, Hon, can you schedule an appointment to see my dentist?" "Say, Hon, can you just pick up a cake on your way home, for Bible Studies tonight?"

At one time, I had a mental schedule for cleaning, paying the bills and balancing our checkbook, planning our meals, house cleaning, cooking, exercising, and family time. I carried a little booklet for my list of things to do, so nothing would slip through the cracks. (I love to check things off my list! Besides helping me be organized, I get a sense of accomplishment at moments when I feel like I have just been wasting time; plus I can check it and see when I called the vet, when I had the car serviced, when I last cleaned the bathtub, or finished a project I was doing for the church.)

A couple years ago, I decided to start using a personal planner (a book, not a person who schedules everything I do). I found one with a pretty cover that brings me joy when I look at it. The advantage of the planner may seem obvious – I now plan specific times to do specific things, instead of merely having items on a list and doing them as time permitted. (The list method was a good way to keep putting off the things I didn't really want to do.) My routine now is to look at my planner every day and keep it up to date. I plan tasks for specific days, but not for the exact time.

You may think this is contrary to the 'One Calendar' idea, but it's not. I check the calendar while filling out my planner and I use a highlighter to mark out times that are already scheduled with appointments or meetings. I know to not schedule anything on Sundays or Wednesday evenings because of church. My planner is a guide for scheduling tasks so I can finish them by a specific date.

When I need to go to the Post Office, I stop on my way home from work. I combine errands that are in the same area of town, but many errands in a row after work can end up taking too long, keeping me away from home later than I want to be. We make it a point to always have family dinner together. (See Chapter 6 – Meal Planning.) In my planner I put a specific date for balancing the checkbook, a schedule for cleaning, a time to work on personal projects (such as writing books, making jewelry, visiting with friends) and I leave time open every day for my family.

I love to use my favorite colors of pens in my planner. Not only does it make it more enjoyable for me to read, I can easily identify the most important items, which I write in bright pink. My favorite things to do are in turquoise, and errands that I need to do outside the house are in purple. I like to use a contrasting color to check off tasks when I finish, and this makes the whole planner journey more pleasant for me. In your own planner, use colors that make you feel good about what you are doing. Or just use one color, or even black, if that's what you like.

For tasks that I hope to do on a specific day but I might not be able on that day, I use sticky notes. Then I can easily move the task from one day to another, and don't have to muck up my planner with correction tape or crossed-out items.

Sometimes, I do not get to my tasks at the scheduled time, which is a good reason to keep some holes in your schedule. At times when I don't feel like doing something that it is scheduled, I look ahead and do a different upcoming task. When I first got the planner, I felt so ambitious, I wanted to fill every bit of time with tasks and projects. I soon learned that I couldn't keep up with my own rigid schedule, and that's okay. As I plan my tasks, errands and duties for the next week, I push forward anything I did not get finished this week. And I leave at least one day each week without planning anything extra (besides Bible study, work, cooking, daily family duties, exercise, and personal care).

If you do not have a photographic memory, use a checklist along with your calendar, or use a planner to help you organize your time. I am astonished at what I have been able to accomplish since I started using a planner.

Organizing your time is an ongoing task that will help you and your family tremendously.

Her children arise up, and call her blessed; her husband also, and he praiseth her.

Proverbs 31:28

6. MEALS! MEAL PLANNING, SHOPPING GUIDE, RECIPES

My grandmother used to say, "What you eat today is how you feel tomorrow." I agree with her. I also noticed that what I eat in the morning affects my whole day.

My mother has a saying, "When an entire family is overweight, it is because of poor eating habits." That includes lack of meal planning.

My husband has a friend who often says, "If you fail to plan, you plan to fail." This includes planning healthy meals.

If you are the family cook, you are the one who manages the health of your whole family when you plan what you all will be eating. What goes into the daily breakfast, lunch, and dinner you prepare makes the difference for your entire family, between being refreshed or tired, being alert or having a foggy mind, maintaining a healthy weight, or gradually gaining every month and every year. This is not a cookbook chapter. I'm providing you with suggestions for organizing and planning your family meals with ideas that have helped me. I find myself spending a good deal of time in the kitchen, preparing food, serving food and cleaning up, so I want to make the most of that time and do as many tasks as necessary while I am there.

We have all heard that breakfast is the most important meal of the day, even for those of us who are not hungry in the mornings (unless I smell bacon cooking – then my stomach starts growling!) I discovered that if I prepare breakfast in the evening, either while dinner is cooking or after dinner, I am more likely to be excited about eating breakfast – and more likely to eat a healthy breakfast. You can prepare the night before and refrigerate: overnight oats (look it up), scrambled eggs loaded with veges or cheese (ready to zap in the microwave), yogurt with fresh fruit, breakfast burrito, bacon, leftovers, even pizza. Ingredients for a smoothie can be stored in a plastic bag and frozen, ready to blend in the morning.

For a sit-down family breakfast, eggs prepared in every way are generally quick to cook. Vegetables can be added to scrambled eggs, fresh fruit can be served on the side with toast and bacon. A cheese enchilada with a fried egg on top is one of our favorites.

My family loves pancakes. I like to use my grandmother's pancake recipe, so I mix up the dry ingredients and divide them into portions in baggies. When we want pancakes, I just add an egg, butter and some milk to the contents of the baggie, mix until lumpy, and drop onto the griddle. (Flip when the bubbles pop.)

As for lunches, I have a coworker who prepares her lunches for the week on Sunday afternoon. She brings healthy lunches every day that smell so good when she heats them in the microwave or toaster oven we have at work. She makes a variation of her Sunday evening meal, or a recipe in the slow cooker, or a stir-fry option, and then she divides it into 5 lunch portions. Maybe you don't want the same thing for lunch every day of the week, but you could prepare 3 portions and intersperse them with something else on the other 2 days. I like to take leftovers from our dinner for my lunch. Find ways to save time in the kitchen by preparing multiple meals at the same time.

You can even prepare a salad the evening before. Put the dressing on the bottom and the salad won't get mushy. When you are ready to eat, flip over the container onto a plate.

When you are preparing school lunches for your kids or husband, you have an advantage if you plan in advance. Some traditional lunch items, such as sandwiches, might be better if they are prepared in the morning, but you can fix them the night before, and include a packet or small container of mustard or mayonnaise they can add at lunch time. When I was growing up, my standard lunch was a sandwich, a piece of fruit, a few chips in a baggie, and a cookie or small desert item – most of which will taste as good if they are prepared the night before, or on Sunday evening. Then only the sandwiches remain to be freshly prepared.

While our daughter was in school, I began saving lunch menus from her district to help me get dinner ideas. This worked well for me, with about 20-25 unique meals each month. Then I started using a blank calendar just for dinner planning, and later, I began using a meal-planning database. We don't always stick to the meal that is on the schedule, but it's a great starting point for those days when you get home and just can't think of what you have on hand.

I had a co-worker who often used her afternoon break to browse through magazines for dinner menus. That seemed like a good idea, but I never got around to it. I sometimes asked my co-workers what they were making for dinner, and that was a good way to be inspired, until many of them started eating fast food every night. I have a lot of cookbooks that mostly sit on my shelf in the kitchen until I want prepare one of the recipes I like to make, but I also look through them at times for more ideas. When I find a recipe I want to prepare at a later date, I mark it with a little sticky note so I can easily find it later. I also have taken photos with my phone camera of my favorite recipes, so I always have them handy. This works well when I want to share a recipe with a friend – I simply email the photo.

Slow cookers are wonderful for people who work all day, especially when you get home late. Another friend, a pastor's wife, prepares every dinner in her slow cooker before she leaves in the morning for work. She gave me so many ideas: a whole chicken or roast with some sliced potatoes, with corn on the cob wrapped in foil around the top of the meat; chopped up beef with onions in water to cook all day, then add a package of frozen vegetables when you get home, so the veges don't get overcooked, for a delicious beef stew; and meat loaf. Did you know you can make your favorite meat loaf in the slow cooker? Two of my other favorites are enchilada casserole and chili.

Remember, salads make great meals when they include protein and a nice variety of yummy vegetables. You can make a delicious, healthy salad at home that rivals those in your favorite restaurant. Why don't we buy spinach leaves or kale or red cabbage? If we include these items in our meal plans, we will buy these items. Add a variety of seeds or fruits (fresh or dried) or cheeses or frozen peas, or any vegetable that will make an appetizing and enjoyable salad. Remember avocados!

These days, we can find dinner suggestions online. I often see Facebook posts asking what others are making for dinner. I sometimes browse meal planning guides on websites, and I have an app on my phone that has a cookbook/meal-planner/shopping guide all in one.

Regardless of how you plan your meals, one great advantage to having your plan in advance, you make your shopping list according to your meal plan. This method is so much better than trying to make meals out of your food on hand. (I wanted to make spinach pie, but I didn't have feta cheese. I hoped to make chef's salad, but I didn't have eggs or ham.) When you go to the store with a shopping list prepared for your upcoming meals, you will be less likely to buy not-as-healthy food on impulse. I think you will also find you are discarding less 'old' food, which saves money and reduces waste.

One great suggestion to save time in the kitchen is to prepare a double-size meal and then freeze half of it for another time. Freezing leftovers works well with lasagna, spaghetti, stews and soups, burritos, pizza, chicken dinners (think Thanksgiving leftovers) and just about everything except salads.

Meal planning can be done weekly, but I prefer to do it monthly, since my weeks seem to go by so quickly. After our meal plan is made, I go grocery shopping twice a month, for fresh milk, bread and eggs, in addition to the ingredients for upcoming meals for the next two weeks.

Get your meals organized, and you will be greatly relieved every day with your plan in place.

She considereth a field, and buyeth it: with the fruit of her hands she planteth a vineyard.

Proverbs 31:16

7. ORGANIZING YOUR OWN SPACE

Did you mother tell you, "A place for everything, and everything in its place"? Mine did. But what happens when every place is filled up and you don't have a place for the new things?

This is the time to do some serious evaluating of what is most important in your life. Do you really need 500 dolls or 200 empty tins cluttering up your space? How do you keep dust off each and every one? Chances are, you don't; it's just too much to maintain. Unless you have room for a huge display case, think about putting away portions of your 'collections.' I am thankful for my own spaces, which consist of one side of the bedroom closet, a dresser, an area beside the bed, and a small office space, which includes another closet. When my own areas are cluttered and I can't find a spot to even set down a book or space for another hanger in the closet, I know I need to get rid of some things.

I recently reorganized the top shelf in the closet by folding all the sweaters I had piled up there, and I selected three that I don't love to donate to the homeless shelter. With that top area looking so neat, and my sweaters displayed in short stacks, I decided to pull out some of my blouses and tops that are not my favorite or don't fit as well as I think they should, so the rest of the closet soon looked as nice and uncluttered as the top shelf. I then expanded to my drawers (does every drawer need to be packed so tightly that it's hard to open? I don't think so) and I ended up filling eight bags with clothes I removed.

I felt so good about getting rid of these clothes that are in great condition yet were just in my way, since I rarely, if ever, wear them. Now my clothes are not so squished together. The act of decluttering my closet and dresser made a big difference in how I felt. I decided to work on my other areas.

The area on my desk around the computer has a tendency to collect items that need action, to be reviewed, or filed. I use a top-of-desk vertical file to sort these items so my workspace can be used for work, and not cluttered with distracting paperwork I don't need to look at right now. (My office space is relatively private, meaning it is in a room where visitors don't go. You might need to be more discreet with your desktop files, especially if your work space is in the dining room.) The files are labeled 'Today,' 'This Week,' 'Maybe Later,' 'To File,' and 'Reference.' These labels are self-explanatory. Each day I go into the office, I check my 'Today' folder and take care of urgent items. I look into 'This Week' to see if anything needs to be moved to 'Today.' I stick papers I might not look at for a while but want to keep handy in 'Maybe Later.' I empty the 'To File' folder once a month by sorting the contents into the file cabinet. I also keep a small box near my desk for papers to recycle.

I keep phone lists of our neighbors and for work, a copy of our Church Covenant and church bylaws, and a booklet of business cards we have received inside the 'Reference' folder, so they are readily available when we need them – handy enough so that when my husband needs a number, he can easily find it, even when I'm at work.

"Say, Hon... do you remember the name of the company who came and cleaned our furnace ducts?" "Look in the 'Reference' folder. His card is in the business card booklet." See how easy that becomes? Instead of searching my brain or online, trying to remember the name of someone who came to our house one time, three years ago, there it is.

Books go on the bookshelf, except when we are reading them. Books do not need to be piled up anywhere in the house. When the bookshelf becomes too full, I scan it for books that can be donated or given to someone in our family. We don't need to keep every book we acquire.

Keeping clutter away from a personal space, either for your clothes, jewelry, make up, books, or computer desk, will help keep away stress, as well as save you time.

> *The Lord is my strength and my shield; my heart trusted in him, and I am helped: therefore my heart greatly rejoiceth; and with my song will I praise him.*
>
> *Psalm 28:7*

8. ORGANIZING YOUR KITCHEN & HOUSE

Do you have the problem of pack-rat-itis, either yourself or a member of your family? Do items appear in your cupboards, so they are constantly bulging at the doors? Does your husband tell you that is merely God's Word being fulfilled, "He will pour you out a blessing that you will not be able to contain," so your garage is packed to the top with items overflowing?

As I mentioned in Chapter 6, you are most likely the one who manages the health of your family by your meal planning and preparation.

In order to be efficient, your kitchen needs to be in order. You need empty counter space available for cutting, chopping, mixing, and sorting; cupboards stocked with food prep, serving and storage essentials, arranged in an organized manner; and a refrigerator and freezer where you can retrieve food without having to remove a hundred other items first. A small amount of weekly maintenance in these areas will eliminate the need for a full-Saturday overhaul.

I am blessed that my husband does some of our family grocery shopping, although many items he purchases are not the types of things I use for cooking or snacking. I designated one cupboard for snacks he buys, and I do my best to not look in there, since I want to avoid eating those types of snacks. I also do not allow cans of soda pop in our kitchen refrigerator – we have a small frig downstairs for pop – because a few cans can quickly fill up every empty slot of my limited refrigerator real estate. When a can or two appears on one of the shelves, I move it downstairs, to its own little frig where it belongs, before it multiplies and those cans with absolutely no nutrition fill spaces that I need for actual food.

We don't like wasting food, do we? We bought it and it's expensive. However, we need to regularly check the refrigerator for expired food and food that is beyond edible. A nurse friend told me, "When in doubt, throw it out." If you can't remember if this container of spaghetti is from last week or the week before, and it still smells okay, you will be safe if you throw it out. Another friend, who is even more efficient with labeling than I am, always writes the name of the food and the date on a strip of masking tape she sticks on the container. She knows without a doubt when a leftover is too old, so she does not waste any time checking: Does it still look okay? Does it smell okay? When did I put this in here? I think it was Monday?

After your kitchen, you have bathrooms, other rooms and closets that need to be organized and stay organized. Bathrooms get the most use in our house, so they seem to get dirtier and messier faster than other rooms.

You are already pressed for time. How can you possibly take care of this monumental task? Use the principle of How to Eat an Elephant: A Little Bit at a Time. Plan to spend 10-15 minutes, perhaps while dinner is cooking, and break down into smaller tasks. Keep the counter tops wiped daily. Clean the floors and mirrors Monday. Organize a drawer Tuesday. Clean a portion of a closet Thursday. Vacuum all carpets one day. (Another blessing is that my husband likes to vacuum and I don't. He takes care of the vacuuming every week and I do the dishes every evening, and that works out well for me. I have a specific way I like our dishwasher to be loaded. "It doesn't matter where you put it. Mom will just re-do it her way.")

We keep our important papers in a file cabinet, and, for some reason, it was in the same condition as my closet and dresser drawers – completely stuffed. Decluttering a file cabinet, for me, is not something I can do in one sitting, so I decided to work on one drawer at a time. Did I need to keep car insurance papers and policies from 10 years ago? What about medical records from 15 years ago? Have I ever looked at them since I put them in the drawer?

Cleaning out the filing cabinet took quite some time, but it was worth it. In my new reorganization, I decided to keep the second drawer, which now stores archives of records, in alphabetical order, while I keep the top drawer in order of 'most recently used.' The folders I frequently use are at the front of the drawer, so I can easily find them. I make labels for all folders – please, clearly label every folder! – so I am easily able to see what I need. I don't think there is such a thing as 'over-labeling.' You will thank yourself later when you don't have to hunt for a folder that either has no label or is labeled in fading pencil or sloppy cursive.

Don't try to do everything in one day. You will get frustrated, and you will never want to organize or clean anything ever again. Small chunks of elephant are easier to digest than the whole thing.

Unfortunately, getting your house organized isn't a one-and-done deal. It's an ongoing chore. You might be looking around at a lot of clutter and feel like you can't get started because everything is already out of control. Just start with one thing, one little area. You will be surprised how much relief you feel after you get started, and that will motivate you do work on the next little area. The rest of your family won't miss the clutter. As a matter of fact, they will be relieved when they can find things so easily! Also, when family, friends, church members and guests come to your home, they will feel welcome and not like another piece of chaos that is crowding up your home.

An organized home is a welcoming home, and even you will feel more welcome after the clutter is gone.

The heart of the prudent getteth knowledge; and the ear of the wise seeketh knowledge.

Proverbs 18:15

9. ORGANIZING YOUR BUDGET

I hope by the time you are reading this, you are not already over your head in debt. If so, I don't have all the answers, except to say, do your best to get out of debt. I suggest that you don't make any major purchases, and pay off your credit cards and other loans using the snowball method (look it up).

In most of the families of pastors I know, more money is spent on church-related items than in other families, whether it be for tithes and offerings, potluck food and snack items, kitchen utensils, church decorations, office supplies, or gas to visit members at home or in the hospital. Another person looking at your budget will wonder why you spend so much in this category, but you know you are doing it to fulfill God's plan, for your husband to get out the Word of God and you to support him in every way you can.

Maybe you and your husband sit down once a month, like my parents did, and go over all your household expenses and pay your bills. Perhaps your husband takes care of all the finances and you don't have to think about them at all. Or, as in my case, the task of taking care of family finances falls on you. This works for us, because I have a mind for numbers and he does not. We discuss major purchases, but the week-to-week and month-to-month organization of our expenses is one of my tasks. We have a combined account, but I prepare the budget and pay the bills. I use a database as our 'check register' (Are you too young to know what a check register is? It's a running balance of our income and expenses in an account), and I spend about an hour each month delegating money to the appropriate creditor and balancing our digital checkbook. We each have a monthly amount of spending money in cash, which we each budget. Since we use cash for most of our purchases, our checkbook is not upset with surprise deductions.

Each month, we set aside a good amount for savings and a portion of our savings is for future credit card purchases. We agree that we don't use credit cards unless absolutely necessary, such as booking a flight, reserving a hotel room, or making a large pre-planned purchase. When we do use a credit card, we pay it off within the week, so we never carry a credit card balance long enough to accrue interest. I believe God is pleased with the money we save by not spending it on interest, and this is only possible by planning our spending and our saving in advance.

This is not a class in budgeting. However, if you don't know how to make and use a budget, I suggest you learn, even if your husband takes care of your household finances. The day may come when you need to know how to do it.

> *Favour is deceitful, and beauty is vain: but a woman that feareth the Lord, she shall be praised.*
>
> *Proverbs 31:30*

10. YOU CAN DO IT!

You may feel like you have a lot of responsibility, and you do. Remember, God is here to help you, to give you strength, hope and joy, as you keep your mind on Him.

Don't think you have to do everything yourself. Ask for help. You will be surprised at how many people are willing to help you with things you think you must do on your own, if you only ask. You can actually make cleaning out the garage fun, if you are working with people who care about you and your time, and the ministry God has given to your husband and you.

This will always be a work in progress, so don't fret if you don't get everything done in one day or one week or one month. As a matter of fact, you will never get everything done – if you did, what would you do?

Schedule time for breaks, time to do what you need to do, time for your family, and time for yourself, even if it's only a little bit. Don't feel like you have to put yourself last. After all, Jesus prayed for Himself.

O Lord our Lord, how excellent is thy name in all the earth!

Psalm 8:9

AVAILABLE FROM EVERLASTING PUBLISHING

BOOKS BY DANA PRIDE

Non-fiction books

Spiritual Enrichment Series

- Say, Hon... The Organized Pastor's Wife

- Following the Way - What Every Christian Teen Girl Needs to Know (with Marilyn Cuffee-Davis)

Steppingstones to Financial Success Series

- Book A: Awareness

- Book B: Budgeting Basics for Beginners

- Book C=D: Credit=Debt

- I Want Ice Cream, Please - Lessons Learned from Our Autistic Son

- My Friend is Deaf

- How to Get Fat Without Even Trying

- What Really Happened in Mexico

- We Choose Our Memories - Sayings of the Young Folks

- We Choose Our Memories - Sayings of the Old Folks

ALSO BY DANA PRIDE

Novels

- Coma Talk

- Vinnie Pinchey

- Hope Continually

- Great Devastation Trilogy
  › After the Great Devastation
  › The Hidden City
  › Immediate Search

- So, How is THAT a Bully?

- The Red Cloak

- Nightmares of Murder

- No One Like You

- Existing

- All These Things

- Kissing a Dead Man

Poetry

- Perceptions of Perfection:
  66 Poems for a Rock Star

Everlasting Publishing
PO Box 1061
Yakima, WA 98907

everlastingpublishing.org

www.ingramcontent.com/pod-product-compliance
Lightning Source LLC
Chambersburg PA
CBHW071851020426
42331CB00007B/1955